Welcome to my world,
You may not know me, but we share the same
emotions. What emotions might you add? Well
heartbreak being one of them. I have cried endless
nights over a love I thought would last a lifetime,
because for some reason at that point in my life, I
knew I had finally gotten it right. I encourage you to
read, read until you can't feel the hurt that you have
been feeling, read until you know you deserve so
much more. This is what this book is about. Not only
did I survive. We survived, which is why we decide
our own VIBES.

–FLO

Disguise

His disguise was everything
Posing as a friend
Only because I kept him in that zone.
He made attempts but none were successful
Little did i know he was the one?

-Flo

Gone Away......

Fighting inner demons
causing you to push away somebody who could
be THERE genuinely.
You've been missing me.
You COULD love me.
You COULD change my perception.
The perception that is no longer of happiness
The thought of giving up comes up.
But not when it had to do with you.
Hearing your heart crying,
only because it can feel me dying.
In denial
Fearful
Stressed
Giving up.
It was ALWAYS happy endings.

Unnoticed

He loves you, But you can't see it
You're too busy going after the one who
doesn't.

11/30/2017

Loving the right person is scarier than loving the wrong person.

Inequivalent

He fucked you to prove to his homeboys he
don't fuck with you.

Circulations

You've created a monster
Telling me you love me
Showing me off
Making me feel wanted
Just to go off and do the same with her.

Thankful

Crazy how comparing your life to somebody else's, makes you realize how good you have it.

Identical

I'm not crying because I miss you
I'm crying because of things you promised me,
I never got them.
Building a relationship with my future
husband,
But now we're strangers.
Somebody who I can walk past and act like I
never met.
The far away kind.
Life throws lemons but I wasn't ready to taste
the lemonade.
I tortured myself
Lying to myself
Praying for you to come back because I didn't
want to feel and deal with that loneliness and
pain that I'm dealing with now.
It's crazy how you are the only one who can
make that go away.
I never liked to revisit this scene.

The one where u dropped my heart from 1000 feet.
But I do it anyways.
I do it with ease.
Just to remind me that I'm good enough for the next bitch nigga.
Just not good enough for him to play me.
It's crazy, you made me.
The person I am.
I love myself way more than you know.
And for that I'm giving my next husband a show.
Hope you search for me in her.
You won't find me.

CPR

I have a problem with falling too fast;
When it doesn't go my way,
I'm left standing with my heart in my hand.
It drips blood and contains no beat.
It's lifeless while I'm trying to find another
man to resuscitate it.
I'm screaming for help
dying because my heart beat decreases.
The ability to love gets worse.
The ability to trust that someone can revive it
gets shorter.
I can't survive this .
I am no longer alive.

Denial

Pretending to not care was the hardest thing I
have ever done

Unworthy

Considering the inconsiderable without
realizing how much you appreciate, how much
he **didn't** appreciate you.
Only to let you be loved by someone else who
was capable.

Appetizer

She's only the other woman
When he's not mad at you.

Unwanted

He was everything you wanted
Until he didn't say "I love you" back.

Rushing

I'm so quick to fall in love, I forget to ask if
that's "what we're doing"

Hiding

Missing you is the hardest
But not knowing if you miss me, is what has
the potential to hurt .

Aftermath

Heartbreak reminds you of why you hate to
fall in the first place.
It wouldn't hurt so bad, if somebody was there
to break your fall.

Labyrinths

Creating an outlet for yourself, u fought your
way in.
A maze that you could barely build.
You made it hard for anybody to get through
to you
and even harder to get through for yourself.
In somebody else's eyes the maze has one exit
and one entrance.
But the one you built has two exits and no
entrance.
Which way would u take if love depended on
it?

Triangle

Trying to impress a guy who wants to be with
the girl that is jealous of you.

Nightmare

You can't make him love you
Stop trying.

Greener Grass

His opinion about you doesn't matter, he is
single for a reason . Remember that!

Depth

Find someone who treats your body well.
Not sexually, But spiritually.
Find someone who wants you to love yourself
more than they will.
Find someone who will genuinely take care of
your well being.

Naïve

You'll believe anything, but won't believe you deserve better.

Humiliated

You didn't protect me but I was the main one
riding for you.
Embarrassment after embarrassment, but you
still chose her.
Lucky her.

Traumatic

It's hard to hide from the pain
When that is all you remember

Disdain

Used my anger and pain for a better purpose
Rather write my feelings than explain them to
somebody who isn't going to listen...

Antidote

Small doses of it might make you sick
which is why you don't need it.
Him.

Unsettle

It only hurt me because I thought we were
All along, we weren't....

Font

Loving and moving on to 1000 dudes
Won't get you that **one** you've been waiting on
only because you're not *his* type.
Don't give up on love. Give up on him.

Effort

I tried my hardest to sleep
But all along you were.
I couldn't help but notice
That the time had ran away
Where do I go?
Since love no longer is available
You don't love me anymore
You didn't even have to say it
It showed.

Facts

Giving him all of you because you think he's
going to stay is the biggest mistake a girl could
ever make
Don't make him a priority without a ring
When he shows the word girlfriend doesn't
mean
Anything

Inspired

Uncontrollable desires to love somebody
You know is not meant for you
The attraction is so real that deep down
You know it's the wrong move
Think about what's best for you

Weary

You created a monster
You spoiled me
Now I can't live with you
But I can't live without you
It makes me sad
It's not like the beginning
It's like we're strangers in the same house
Loving that we ignore each other
I love the way you turn your back
And you love the way I nit pick
Why are we?
What are we?
How are we?

Secure

Spending her time getting to know him,
while he's wasting her time.

Laceration

He's lied to you multiple times
"He's never been with her"
She came to you as a woman
You blew it off because you didn't want to
believe
Then you seen the pictures
It was worth 1000 words.
Do you believe now?

Resentment

I smile at the fact that you look for me in her.
Imitation is the best form of flattery.

Undeserving

If he chooses women who aren't on your level,
This just means he's not on yours either.

Virus

It eats at my soul
It tells me I'm unworthy
It also makes me trust.
I can't help but to attempt to indulge.
Not knowing how bad I want or need it
Not knowing what bad comes from it
I Fein
I prey
Not on my hands and knees
The kind that steams from wanting more
Can you guess?
Love.

Modify

Creating an atmosphere you would love to live in, even if you didn't create it.

Discerning

In relationships we remember everything, but
what we did wrong

Harass

Don't nag about him mistreating you
When you ultimately choose to stay

Folly

Accepting apologies for the same mistakes
is a never ending cycle of betrayal.

Licentious

He has several different women
You're not different.

Panorama

You loved him so much
That the excuses you made for him
were becoming your truth about him.

Gold Digger

She missed out on everything spiritually
Because she looked for it materialistically
Money can't buy you anything worth having.

Forbidden 7

The coworker I always wanted
Handsome, chocolate, masculine
We always locked eyes
But we never once spoke
When he did speak it was a turn on
The simplest questions made me answer
quickly
Only because I was too shy to ignore him
The depth of our conversation ruled out every
argument.
I looked down and there it was the ring that
he deserved.
Too curious for my own good.
Wonder how his lips taste? ....

Forbidden 6

It was Valentine's Day
I made her dinner
I brought her flowers
Roses to be exact
We ate, made love and watched movies
I had to run to take an important phone call
It was her, the one I had been waiting on
Meeting her at our place
I walked up to the door
My kids answered "happy Valentine's Day
Daddy"
My wife greeted me with a card and bear
To tell me how much she appreciated me .

Forbidden 5

She was everything I wanted and more
She never compared to the daily routine I had
She was confident
Sexier
Caring
Understanding
She never nagged
Until one day I couldn't see her
Because I was having dinner with my wife
Ignoring messages
Explaining to my wife it was my job
Lying .

Dubious

Sitting alone listening to slow jams that match
your mood.
Wishing that you could turn your fantasies
into reality.
Waiting on your Ken doll to show up with
flowers for no reason.
Wanting somebody to want you because you
want them.
Hoping love isn't hiding from you,
Even though you have been hiding from it.

Reflection

You have convinced him that you are the one
for him to a point where you can't even be
yourself.
You're different
You've changed
Look in the mirror
Do you even see yourself anymore?
Or do you see his woman?
Don't neglect yourself

Relentless

Tell her you love her
Show that you need her
Before your good woman
Finds a good man

Karma

Sex was the only pro
He never fed my spirit
He only wanted what made him **feel** good
Regardless of how I put **it** down
It was never enough
It was always **her**
Somebody who didn't even care
I hope you fall in love with her
I hope she treats you right
So when u come back to me
You can feel that same knife.

Consistency

Everything you do
He does the opposite
That's not 50/50

Heartbroken

Causing so much pain
Causing you to blame yourself
Making excuses as to why you shouldn't be
loved
Making you wish he'd had never left
It wasn't your fault
You should have loved him more
These are the things we say, when we don't
want to accept .
Trust your instinct
Cry
It's okay to hurt
Heal yourself

Bitter Sweet

U been sipping this whole time
Not knowing what it's doing to you
Causing wrinkles
Stressing you out
His love doesn't taste that good .

Euphoria

I don't want to scare you
But I just trust you
Too sober to believe it's fake
Your love is a high I can't come down from
At this point you're not too high to reach
You're just too low to touch
I love everything about you
It's a bad trip
Remember.

Fruitful

May your mind wonder, to a place you don't
belong
To ease the pain, from every wrong
To hold your heart & heal your wounds that
were planted by those who abandoned your
tree.
Water yourself.

Kept

Before you do anything
Make sure he wants to stay first.

Occurrence

To be involved, you have to evolve.
Think about it.

Impart

Realizing how good you were to them
Realizing how bad they were to you
Compare and contrast
Evolve.

Cognizant

When u realize it's in front of you ,
It will be everything you want && then some.

Proofreading

Just think of how hurt you would be if everything would have WENT the way u hoped!

Ashamed

You made it real easy for me to walk away
And I made it real easy for you to stay
What now?

Set UP

Ignoring your messages
Calling you throughout the week
But suddenly it stops over the weekend
Late night invites to chill
But no day dates
Don't ignore the signs
He's playing you.

Off Guard

I trusted you with my heart
You never trusted me
Maybe that's why I'm never receiving
The love that I think I deserve.

Seek

My kisses write a list of things I love about
you.
While your eyes can see everything you love
about
me.

Attractive

Look at me like you never want to lose me .
It counts.

Severe

You sat in the love seat and got disrespected instead.
Just because you remain seated, won't make the seat more comfortable.

Self Worth

Making plans and building a life with somebody who doesn't even see themselves in my life . He doesn't deserve me.

Wronged

She was my best friend
My day one
Jealousy was her greatest characteristic
She laughed and joked with me
Only to find out that she loved **him**
Why does it hurt so bad?
he belonged to me.

Low Key

He surprised you with his lips
His kisses was intense
Never thought this day would come
He makes you feel special
Only because he wants you
But not the way you think it's going to keep
him
Ignore him
It's not worth it

Evasive

Angry because you let him hurt you
But happy because he hasn't left yet
Don't confuse how you have been treated
With what you deserve.

Convenient

You were the greatest potential I had ever
seen

Credit

The problem is, you're putting too much time into someone who doesn't deserve the love you have to offer.

Barbies Dream House

Creating a reality for yourself
Based off of the love you dreamed about
The scenes were scripted
Just like his love for you...
beware...

Usual

You're so hurt
Only when hurt becomes normal
You don't realize you're hurt until you're hurt.

Temperature

My heart is freezing
I can't grip the door to let you in.

Questions

I asked you that one question
U offered your aggression
Which quickly silenced love at sight.
How could you love her?
What do u see in her?
Why does she bring out the best ?
You said this was a test of my true affection
I completely failed with the rest

Pressure

I loved the worst part of you
Even though you only showed the worst part
to me.

Complacent

Being with you was so common and hurtful
It's makes being away so difficult

Intoxicated

I'm trapped in between missing you
and loving the fact that you're not around.

Mistaken (his perspective)

I loved her,
but lost me.

Forbidden 4

What would she think?
I ran off and did something terrible
I didn't mean to
The night was so young
She tasted so good
But now we're expecting
Two little hands, two little feet
I can't be the man of the house
Because that isn't my house
What should I tell my wife?
She would die
Please don't leave me......

Forbidden 3

I watched her sleep
Dreaming out loud
Wondering if she would ever find out
I shower to rinse the scent away
Just so it wouldn't hurt her
The smell of another woman would kill her
I love her.

Broken Clocks

I got too comfortable,
I sent my feelings through a text
You didn't respond
Which let me know the feeling wasn't mutual.
I asked if it was something wrong with me
Because when I turn around there is always a
"she"
Who knew it would hurt this bad
Who knew the pain would strike
You chose her over me and I thought I was
Mrs. Right
She doesn't even love you
Not even as good as me
What did I do to deserve the cold you
When I gave u love when u needed me.

Bliss

The silence between us
Is more awkward than usual
Not knowing the words to say
But we know we're wrong
Fixing all the problems that we don't have
Just to ignore the fact that we do have them
I still
He still
We still
Are we?

Low Carb

Don't feed my heart what you know it needs,
then turn around and starve me.

Citation

Rewinding time to specify the present
Only to be selfish with my destiny
All to be with somebody who won't even
marry me.

Buried alive

I used the shovel you gave me to dig up my
heart
Just to find you holding it

Anguish

And the scary part is, I almost died loving you.
All the while, you never lived loving me.

Deceit

He was known for being promiscuous
But I loved it
The attention I got from females was my joy
As females threw themselves at him, I laughed
He only paid me attention
I had to be careful
Until one Day she came
Knocking at my door
Crying hysterically about how he beat her
She told me to be careful
It was more than I could imagine.
The pain, the deceit.
I could hear her heart
When I should have been hearing my own.

Inexcusable

I hated the fact that she loved him
The more they were seen together
The more I was uncomfortable
I wasn't jealous
I wasn't mad
I was curious
As to what he thought she was
She wasn't me
I wasn't her
But I assumed I was better
I was prettier
More energetic
Natural......

Drained

Teaching myself how to love you was the
hardest, but teaching you how to love me was
the easiest.
Only because I didn't need much and you
needed it all.

War

I left
And that was my hardest accomplishment

Realize

They say you're hard to love
But to them , THAT excuse makes it easier
to push you away.

Tenses

Is it possible to miss something you never had?
Is it possible to love something you never missed?
The empty feeling inside when you're lonely is like a cosmic high you can't come down from.
You wonder if you have met "HIM"
The "what if's"
The "should"
The "woulds"
The times you had his back & the second he breaks your heart you turn around to see if he has yours....
You wonder if he still cares
You wonder if "he" was "him"
To make sure, you got another glimpse of the past from which HE HAD, YOU DID, YALL DIDN'T, and YOU ARE.
You are lonely
You are hurt
You are enraged
And it's okay.

Monster

Unwilling to love
Unwilling to venture out and get to know
myself
Don't want to learn you.
Only to protect myself from disappointments
Protecting myself from people who prey on
good spirits, that love hard and own the label
"handle with caution"
He's constantly looking for me
Searching high and low
Yearning for me
Attempting to change my heart
You won't
I''ll fight it
The aggression of past heart ache won't let
you win
There is no love, so cold, so empty
Broken pieces,
Missing pieces, so you can't put it back
together
I'm tired

He's tired
He looks at me with sorrow
"What are we doing?"

Played.

His friends laugh because he thinks he's king
He tells you you're beautiful
Behind the scenes he fiends
He will never know the kind of love you hold
Simply because he wasn't man enough
He gloats about your sexual escapades
And how you're so good in bed
But really deep down he wants to be your
married man
He puts on this facade like he's a player
All the while you fall in love with his best
friend
Only because his best friend was the one who
showed he cared.....

Rejected

I hold back so much, only because I want to
keep it all in.
I keep tabs to see if he's watching.
I make arrangements to fit his schedule
It's hurts when he doesn't look my way
He won't pay attention to me
Only because he's not interested
I crave him
All the while he doesn't crave me.
What's now.

Changes

You've been ashamed for too long
You know it's time to change
But you're so scared that you may forget who
you really are
Change is for the better
Don't be complacent
You won't forget who you are
You will be glad , because it made you who
wanted to become .

Husband

Hardworking
Trying to feed his family
He wants more for his life
But can never get ahead , only because the
minor set backs are pushing him to the edge .
He smiles when it hurts
His pain runs deep.
He needs me to rub his feet
Keep him afloat
To steer the boat or ship that helps us gets
pass the times we had a major slip.
I have to love him
I have to motivate or he won't protect
In order for this to work it can't be just based
on sex.

Forbidden 2

He calls blocked & I answered
Figuring out the right times late night
I'm anxiously waiting for him to meet me
He caresses my body because it feels right
The regret I feel with every kiss
The remorse I have with every touch
It's not right
It's 5am and his wife calls...

Caution

When she pushes you away that means come
closer.
Everybody expresses love differently.
Hers was just at a distant
Only to maintain the parameters of pain.
She didn't know your soul.

Facade

Confused on what you really want
Only because you see what social media
provides
He made mistakes hoping she would stay
It never dawned that hurting her was only
pushing her away
Breathe
Think
Hold it together
He's empty like the trash she threw his ring in
Slamming doors
Cussing and fighting
Leaving
Seemed like nothing was ever going to change
She stayed , even tho the pain wouldn't go
away
&& he so comfortable
Stayed the same .....

Despite

You have destroyed every aspect of love that I
ever imagined was good,
And yet here I am, still loving you like you love
me back.

Motionless

Secretly looking for a way out
The same way that got me in.
In too deep to feel
In too deep to be real
Feel every inch
Express every thought
Craving the rush
Preying on the urge .
Trust the feeling.

Conditional love

He stopped pretending to love you because the terms, conditions and agreements were up.

Mysterious

He is a mystery one you can't figure out
He laughs at awkward times
He smiles with beautiful teeth
He talks with so much confidence
There's so much i want to know
I want to know his soul.

Lost

As the darkness tucks you in at night
You lay awake with tears
The ones you shed for many reasons
Some you did with fear.
It's crazy how we wind up,
We look and shake our heads
Our life is suppose to be beautiful
But every day we dread.
Depressed
Confused
Hurt
Happy
It all starts running together
We don't know which emotion to play
Just the cards the life have dealt us

Cheating

You said you'd leave
You never let him treat you that way.
You craved the attention
He craved her
You cried
He tried.
Every moment of sadness you endured was
like a trophy for him.
A trophy for the time he cheated.
A trophy for the time he left
A trophy for the day you left
He left you speechless
He left your mind naked
Wondering.

Jealousy

You stalk her page
You wait for them to break up
Simply because you haven't let go of the past
"What does he see in her?"
"Why didn't he love me"
Be glad you weren't the chosen one.
Simply because the chosen one , was purposely
chosen to get her heartbroken.
She tosses and turns effortlessly hurting and
crying
Be grateful the burden was not yours.
The things we hope for aren't meant for us ,
because it's suppose to save your heart from
pain.
You're meant for something GREATER

Warrior

Scared of success
Afraid of failure
Contemplating your next move
Needs support but doesn't need the extra
comments
She laid here daydreaming wishing to turn her
dreams to reality
Oh the damage her mind could do
She loved herself hard as if it was the last love
she would ever experience
She was drowning in fears
Fears that weren't anything but a facade of
what she wasn't suppose to have in life .
Keep playing the game babygirl.

Avenue

He took her hand
Even when she didn't have it out to hold
To simply guide her to her heartache
To confront it
She let go because she wasn't ready to face the
truth
It was too deep
The scars she had spent time abandoning were
resurfacing
She couldn't handle it
Her heart was beating faster and faster as
they inched forward.
She began to break down
Wanting to turn around and run
But he clinched her hand harder
He whispered he loved her and her vision was
clear
She cried and bent down
Wondering what happened to her.
Simply staring at how she has changed
She realized heartache changed her

Dramatically.
She didn't recognize herself.
Don't be that girl.

Meant

You were meant for something more than this
Laying alone awake at night
Fighting all the demons
They never stop
The pain
The tears
Like waves, but only you can hear them.
Only you can be the barrier through pain and
joy within yourself.
Sometimes we get so caught up we forget we
even have one.
And before it's too late, somebody has already
walked in the room you didn't want them to
notice, your barrier is gone.
The room is dark, and feels like heartbreak.
U can smell the fear in the air
only because it's coming from you.
Afraid to love, let loose, and be happy.

Soul mating

The way we connect our bond was unbreakable we finished each other's sentences without problems you changed my heart. you made me feel that feeling. the feeling you get when you're comfortable in a bed the feeling that catches you by surprise it makes you over look flaws the kind of "love at her first sight" feeling

The feeling that makes you love harder than anything before. you care so much that the thought of losing that person makes you sad instantly. its knowing that person is for you. not by horoscope, not by coincidence, but by feelings.

The feeling grabs you like a warm summer day it makes you want to never love anybody else. it's like your souls are touching and they match. it's like an everlasting scribing for the same soul you been waiting on all your life you instantly want to marry this person. You instantly plan a life. you don't understand it?

feed back is indescribable, it' not something forced. when they are gone, you can't compare nor replace it with anything else.
your soul is matched.
when its ruined, you wait patiently for another soul mate

Timing

Never explain your situation
Ignore negativity
Elevate your mind to the point where what
other people say can't harm you.
Everything comes when it's suppose to
Especially in the sense of timing
Your greatness prowls down when need be
Your enemies will fall to your feet
Jealousy will be given like a compliment on a
nice summer day.
It won't faze you due to the amount of level-
headedness you will experience.
Congrats you are what you never thought you
would be

Wading

One day the love you been searching for
Is going to come looking for you
Saying "THERE YOU ARE"
Be patient.

Elevate

The amount of pressure you hold in
The amount of pain you gained
The way you move is successful
Explore the art behind your waves
You think that you have lost buy really it's
your confidence
It sneaks behind you telling you to run away
Don't leave
You argue back , fight for yourself
Know your worth, every inch of pain and
struggle
Create an atmosphere so dope that you don't
want to leave.
Elevate your mind
Love your flaws
You're ready.

Souled Out

Missed calls.
Unanswered texts
Pending emails
Those are signs you love him
Just not enough to keep hurting yourself
Why hold on to what you need to let go of?

Horoscope

Wishing , hoping and praying he comes back
Reminiscing on the good
Where did we go wrong?
Where did I go wrong?
Preparing the speech you'll never get to give
Coming up with words
Expressing emotions you didn't think existed
Just to continue to plan a life you don't even
know that you're going to get.
It never gets better
The feelings get suppressed as the days go on
Waiting on a ring you thought you deserved
from the person you thought he was
He's to blind
He's too arrogant to say sorry
You don't even need much
You just need him to say 3 words

Damage

U loved the wrong person whole heartedly.
Imagine how amazing the love will be when
you love the right person whole heartedly.

Abuse

She looked in the mirror
She cried about the person she had become
Am I worth it?
She was simply seeing what he saw
Scared of his hands
Confused on if they hated or loved
So lost.
Scared to leave
Confused on Love
"He must really love me."

Antisocial

Her tears are yelling at you to get your shit
together.

Nothing major

You're too pretty to cry, adjust your crown..
It's just spilled milk

Sexual healing...

Lay me down
Undress me
Not just taking my clothes off
Undress me with your mind
Undress me with your heart
Reveal your hearts mind .
Rub me
Feel my emotions run through your fingers
Make love to my spirit
Kiss my soul
Pretend I'm the prettiest emotion you have
ever seen
Love me gently
Light as a feather but hard as a rock
Match my soul sexually
Mentally
Physically
Sex me.

Attention

You're excited
It's something new
The feeling is fresh
The conversation has grew
You start thinking about little things
Relationships
Love
Marriage
You talk everyday getting to know this person
Your wondering what is their flaw
Meanwhile you never really notice how much
this person made a difference until you don't
talk anymore
It's easy to become attached when all you
wanted was that one thing
It completes you for the time being && almost
never goes away
We crave it in every way , good or bad .
You smile because you get it
It makes you feel this way.
Alive

Happy
With no worries

Unconditional

She loved him so much she forgot about
herself.

Unyielding

I fell in love with what I thought he was
Not what he showed me
I was loyal to where I thought his loyalty was.

Unresolved

I ran away to prove a point
Now i am struggling to find my way back
I proved that i could handle this feeling
But failed to realize how much it would hurt
to run away.

Ulterior Motive

I hope you fall for her just like I fell for you
Just so she can break you
So I can help piece you back together

Let Go

U still love him
U watch his page
U wish he would come back
And prove that everything he had done was
wrong.
You want him to admit to hurting you.
U want him to love you again
But what your heart wants is not what it
needs.
It needs consistency.

Killing the Cat.

I am only curious because I can't have him.

Forbidden...

I smelled your cologne on my work clothes
I washed your lips off mine
These days have become to common for us .
I don't belong to you .
Your lips on my neck get me every time
Your hands on top of mine
How do I stop this rollercoaster from derailing
without killing us?

Selfish

Don't feel bad for dating him.
Just because they had a bad experience.
doesn't mean you will.
He is different around you , than he was with
her.
Cherish him.
Love him.
Experience love.
It only comes around every so often.

Distance

Don't you hate when distance is the reason
you can't love someone the way you need to.

Instinct

People aren't use to things they can't control
The feeling of being desired by the undesirable
was the best
His voice calmed me
His hands soothed me
He made me think that love existed.

Incredible

Everything about him was sensible.
His conversation was immiscible
I loved the way he spoke
brought joy to my soul.
The way he laughed spelled love in bold.

Anticipation

The kisses from the back sent chills down my
arms.
Waiting patiently for him to come to my
room and take charge .
He kisses my thighs which made me relax.
He kissed my forehead and I waited on him to
make another move.

Crash

Even though u don't love me back.
I can't always act like I don't yearn for that.
Even though you see me as someone you'd
never love, I'll never stop trying to be real.
Only wanting to feel your lips against mine
But I refrain from crying because you honestly
loved her more.
All I wanted was affection
Along with protection
The type you need not with just sex.
I wanted to be wanted by the one who never
wanted me
in the beginning just friends.

Alone

She loved him until she didn't love herself
anymore.
She was lost .
She was abandoned.
She was confused on how something that
begged for her attention could hurt so much.
She fell in love with love.
Forgetting what the actions felt like.
Sitting in silence, waiting on him to love her
back.
waiting on anybody to love her back.
She needed it
She wanted it.
She would do anything to know what love was
The silence spoke louder than words.
There was nothing, empty, alone, scarce.
Dreaming about love became more of her
reality than her fantasy.
She remains laying in bed at night with no
insight on how love feels.

Unbelievable

Begging for my attention until I grew fond of you.
Now you are this person I have never met before.
Where did you go?
What did you do to him?
Why can't I find him?
How do I find something I never lost?

–Flo

Choose

My pain runs deeper than you think
The way you touch me
The way you feel me
The kisses on my neck make me not want to
speak
I figured you was one of them fly niggas
Those stunting ass niggas in the street.
Make a bitch feel comfortable enough and rub
her feet
Once I laid eyes on you, there was no turning
back ,
U was everything I wanted and more with the
"ring to match".
We laughed , we joked, we kissed , we spoke
about real things that were incomparable to
real conversation.
Had me guessing and wanting to know if you
felt the sensation, to make me ya girl and
have relations.
You finessed me into thinking you were feeling
me and the feeling was definitely mutual.

We locked eyes.
I cried and told you I didn't care about the materialistic shit in life .
The end result of the situation is never good.
I'm too good to settle for just as friends.
It's funny becuase I always fall for the same type and get hype about shit that just looks good. It never dawned on me that we could never be and never would.

Insanity

If that man loves you, actions speak louder
than words
We fall for shit we think has potential
But in real life it's just an everlasting fantasy.
You can talk all day but actions mean more.
You can hold my hand and still love whores.
You can kiss me goodnight but not want sex
Doesn't mean you don't lay with me thinking
about the next.
Females minds be so emotionally fucked
Only because all we want is love
We trust
We listen
We fight
We argue
But when it's all said and done the man is still
in charge .
Only because she is willing to give up
everything for that four letter word she may
or may not get.
It's crazy because I can relate .

Running around after a nigga you secretly
don't want to hate.
He loves me "we say"
He won't hurt me "we say"
But all the while loving and fucking the next
bitch not thinking about the consequences to
his actions or the consequences to your heart.
Nobody is loyal, everybody wants what you
got?
The epitome of a relationship that's built on
unstable blocks!
I can't stand to see myself hurt but yet I keep
him around. Repeating the same cycle
expecting a different outcome but the same
one is found.

Struggle

My demons are haunting me.
The day you left was the day they came alive
I tried to warn myself in the beginning
You were not worth a cry .
The tears I had every time you crossed my
mind.
Should I keep trying?
For somebody who claimed they love me.
How is it that easy to pick up and go.
I limited myself on life with you
And now I feel as though I'm drowning.
All I ever wanted was to make you happy.
But instead you did the opposite to me.
The pain, the hurt, the disappointment.
Every day was a struggle to think about how u
didn't deserve me.
How you didn't earn me.
The worst part about this, it's not your fault .
It's mine.

Healing

Everything you have thought of about him is
out there; just don't give up on parts of him.

Risk

Stop going through his phone.
Your relationship is already over!
The half truth is something that you have been
Believing for sometime now. The erased text
messages
The arguments with random girls, he's
disrespectful and entertaining the people who
you would turn away. It's not the same. You
lying at home alone , seeing the potential, but
the only potential you see is in the Hennessy
bottle that you got you feeling this way in the
first place. don't be naive they say, don't take
him back they say. Time heals all wounds, but
you can't heal something when it's
continuously being torn open by the same
individual you keep trying to get to close it.
Time to let go. Stop looking for potential.

HIM

Maybe I'm crazy.
Maybe I'm blind.
Why don't we see eye to eye?
It's like I'm invisible or maybe you're invisible too?
Why haven't I found you?
All I ever wanted was to meet you.
Make you mine
Kissing you from head to toe
Riding your dick in slow mo'
Making love all night like I'm your wife
And every time you slap my ass
It's your lips I bite.
It's crazy I haven't met you yet, it's like we live in opposite worlds.
I search and search and I can feel your ora.
But every time I think too hard I know I'm dreaming.
It's like we met before but I don't know what to expect.

You make me happy in my dreams and I know that's respect.

I can't even complain about NOT having a man,

It's like we cuddle every night and don't regret it.

Everybody asks who u are and I tell them you're HIM

BUT HOW do I know if I'm her when I'm still waiting?

Scared

The thought of losing you was always on my
mind
Even then I didn't want to think about it.
Everything about the relationship seemed
genuine
My purpose for life was you and the thought
of us
I cared too much until one day the pain never
stopped
I thought it would be over because the air you
had breathed was no longer existing around
me.
I was scared to be alone
Scared to know anything other than you.
The fear of knowing you had somebody else
The fear of thinking she was prettier than me
The fear of my reality becoming fantasy
Everybody wants to be like the movies and
instagram
Showing off the "love" they have that seems
perfect

I prayed for God to let me know if you were
my soul mate
Instead it's been a month with no phone call
and no answers. No letters like before.
It must feel good to become strangers.
To be strangers with somebody you loved.

Recognize

Take care of her soul.
Make love to her mind,
Cherish her body.
Love is the easiest part.

Rich

Searching for him in another man, but always disappointed because I am unable to find someone to do me so wrong.

Feelings

You never face them, only because of the mood they put you in.
You're scared to go there. Who can blame you??

-Flo

Amour

The late night "can I see you?" text.
Remember he is not yours.
-Flo

Acidic

He speaks rough, his mannerisms show.
You like the tough act. It turns you on.
Until it's not an act anymore.
He mistreats you.
You're blinded by wanting a "bad boy", you have
chosen to be okay and settle.
Don't steer away from what u deserve.

-Flo

Word Play

Confusing lust with love will have u chasing a boy
instead of a man
And girl instead of a woman
And have u loving materialistically instead of
emotionally
What can they do for me?
The most selfish question, always followed by a selfless
answer
Only a real minded person can decipher the damage
that can be done when both words are used
interchangeably.
Beware.

Resentment

Regretting the day I met you
Wishing I would have never taken the steps
Realizing how much you were a burden.
Moving forward as the strangers we had become.

-Flo

Better

If he mistreats you, it's not going to change just because he has someone new. He has to want it for himself baby girl. You were just a part of the cycle.

-Flo

Intimate

You touched my back, which gave me chills.
You caressed my back and breathed in my ear.
You turned me over, so you could fit perfectly.
It took my breath
I never knew something so gradual would feel so good.
We were finally one.
I never wanted to let you go.
I couldn't let you proceed.
We crossed that boundary
I'm here. Waiting
Waiting on something that might not ever happen.
For us to be "us".
Are we ruined?

–Flo

Dream Catcher

He lies behind you at night because he wants to hear
your dreams.

-Flo

20/20

I cried and you didn't care
I left and you watched me
It was clear you had moved on
It just hurt actually "knowing" that for sure.

−Flo

Relinquished

Finishing what you started, because it was better
than abandoning the one you thought loved you.
Full of regrets but you can't turn back.
Hiding
Not only physically but emotionally.
Done.

-Flo

Commitments

I don't want a ring for the title of "marriage".
It shows that you believe I am your best friend and
you are willing to love and crown me forever as
yours;
Queen.

-Flo

Tally marks

I created you
I built you
I respected you
Can you name three things you have done for me?

Infatuation

I ran right into his arms , only because you pushed
me .
You had no intentions on doing good.
You left me weak
I watered you
Made you whole
Separated the good from the bad and never told the
bad.
You know my secrets
And I know yours
The possibility of "us"
What about the love ?
It's gotten deeper than that
You have created a monster
Not the scary kind
The kind that doesn't love herself anymore
The kind who will sabotage your next relationship
Only because you won't listen
Then you turn around and call her crazy
Yes thank you .
Scorned.
And you wonder why she looks at you with despair

She is hurt .
She is crushed .
She is me .

FriendZone

Going to sleep I long for you to touch me.
Make me feel so good that I can't go to sleep without it.
I love the feeling of your lips
Your breath on my neck while you're in it
The sound of your moans turns me on.
I get excited thinking about you between my legs
They shake when I think about how warm your body feels next to mine.
It's hot.
But my heart is cold.
I want it.
I need it.
I fantasize about it.
I want to hear you say it's mine.
You can't because it is forbidden.
We are "friends" remember.

Refreshing

Looking back on the past to see if it upsets me. Don't
be burdened.
I am extremely happy you left.
It was the biggest thing you could've done.
I love better without you.

Untitled Vibes

Hope you enjoy.

-Flo

I have a problem.
Letting you in wasn't it.
Letting you love me was.
The fact that you had me spiraling out of control;
To attempt to love you the way I wanted to be loved.

It comes with warning signs
Caution here
Don't enter there
But you do it anyways
And you always end up hurt.
Love.

You got me
I'm wide open
In my feelings the way you want me
I'll do anything to be with you
I'll surrender everything,
To get nothing in return.

I changed purposely
Only for you to recognize I wasn't the girl
you wanted.
I begged you to stay
But instead you pushed me away
Away from the clouds
The clouds that are currently raining on my
heart.
Tears couldn't compare
They drown me.
You remain to be the only one who can void my
soul of all the water.
Through it all I'm able to stay afloat.

I've been comparing his love for me
To his love for her
It's not the same.
I'm open .Bare. Naked
This is how he wanted me
And now I'm here.
Stop my tears.

I created boundaries for you to follow
Just to make excuses to break them.
I'm in love with you

It's okay to admit that you miss him
It won't deem you dumb or stupid
It just means you have feelings && that's ok.

I'm running scared
Hiding
Ducking
Dodging
Just to get away from the feeling
I don't want to feel
When I feel it hurts
I felt you love me
&& that was the worst feeling ever only
because I knew that once that feeling was
gone
It would never come back
It would be kidnapped
Taken from me
Leaving me
Leaving my heart
Crying and lonely
Yet I took a chance
I gambled everything
Now my heart is up for grabs
I wish yours was, so I could bet on it. I
miss you.

Why is love so hard to have, so easy to give
& so easy to lose?

Fake like you love me
Just so they can see my worth
I need you to want me
Even though you don't
You complete me in ways you don't see
I can't see when you're away
Imagine you gone from me
I would lose my breath
The way you kiss me keeps my heart beating.
You keep me alive
Just knowing you're there is the reason I
continue
I'm in too deep
To deep to stop
So deep that I cry at the thought of losing
you
If I lose you I would lose myself
Do you understand now?
I can't live without you.

You blame him for putting you second,
Yet you play the role so well.

I've asked God to bring you **back** to me & every
time. I end up crying more and more.

You create the love that you wish you could receive which makes you special.

You're too independent
You're too self sufficient
He won't notice you.
He won't have anything to do with you
He's intimidated
And honestly he's not good enough to handle
what you can handle baby girl.
And that's okay. There is better.

Be her reason she will love again.

-Flo

Love her so she doesn't become bitter

-Flo

She was his backbone. She was the reason....

-Flo

I am always his never.

-Flo

I would settle for an "I miss you" right now.

-Flo

Y'all play and waste time, knowing the
feeling is mutual.
You want him. Admit it.

-Flo

I have created this wall. You aren't allowed
in. And it's not allowed out.
My heart.

-Flo

Talent;
Nobody can take that from you.

-Flo

He hurt you so bad; he made you love yourself
more than he ever has.

-Flo

I Harbor so much hurt, but yet I still have
this love that continues for you.

-Flo

You stay awake at night, because you know
that if you are left alone, you will break
down. And that's the worst feeling ever, to
feel broke down.

-Flo

If you have to "wonder", he is not yours.

-Flo

I dream about him. But yet he hasn't showed
up yet. The man of my dreams.

-Flo

The best love comes in fantasy form.
Fairytales.

-Flo

Love him so he won't give up.

-Dorsey

inspired by Flo